HOW TO DEA GASLIGHTING

RECOGNIZE AND STOP HIDDEN PSYCHOLOGICAL MANIPULATIONS AND ABUSE

Bob Scott

Copyright

Printed in the United States of America

© 2019 by Bob Scott

Double Portion Publishers

USA | CANADA

Table of Contents

Introduction

The term 'gaslighting' originated from a novel: a mystery thriller written in 1938, but has now become a solid part of the English vocabulary. Gaslighting is a form of psychological manipulation in which a person (the gaslighter) subverts another person's reality by denying obvious truths, the surrounding environment, or their feelings. People targeted by gaslighters will, in turn, go against the very basic instincts they possess—they will no longer trust their perception, awareness, emotions, or who they are.

Let's say a young woman tells her boyfriend that he is not tending to her emotional needs by spending all his free time with his drinking buddies but the boyfriend did not even accept that the situation exists, he is gaslighting her.

Gaslighting is more common than you would want to believe or imagine. It is so insidious, so subtle that unless you know the things to look out for, you may not even realize that you are being gaslighted until the damage is done. It can affect your emotional, psychological, and physical health if left unresolved.

While any gender could be gaslighted, women are more susceptible to it. Scientific articles as old as the early 80's put forward the hypothesis that because women were brought up in a way that makes them to desire and hunger for human connections, they are more susceptible to getting exploited as a result of this need.

Gaslighting can hardly occur in a relationship between two equals. But in a relationship where one party has a form of power or influence over the other, it is very easy for gaslighting to exist. It may be a romantic relationship where one partner is more in love or more powerful than the other, or it could be between family members (parents-child, sibling-sibling, relatives), or other non-familial relationships (bosses, mentors, friends). A person that has given the other party power over them is afraid to ask questions and can be gaslighted quite easily. It is a tool favored by abusers, cult leaders, narcissists, and any other group that enjoys exerting control on other people.

The goal of a gaslighter is to gradually erode the victim's belief in themselves, their reality, and decisions. And because gaslighters are very good at putting up a convincing act. The victim gradually begins to accept what they are told over what is real. The victim stops trusting themselves or starts questioning what they believe to be true. It will then get to a point where the victim finds it easier to accept whatever the gaslighter says as truth.

CHAPTER 1: How to Spot a Gaslighter

If there is an attribute that gaslighters seem to have in abundance, it is charm. They are generally likable people that seem to ooze oodles of charm and this may make it difficult to identify them on the surface.

There are, however, some manners of behavior by which they can be identified and these include:

1. **Withholding:** Here the gaslighter withholds knowledge of what they know or what is fact by pretending not to understand their victims. They may begin sentences with phrases like ''Are you trying to confuse me by...?'' or ''Please, don't come with this again. Haven't I told you...?'' It is a tactic to disorient the victim by making him/her feel like they are wrong or misunderstood a situation.

2. **Countering:** The victim's facts are made to be false as victims are blamed for their 'forgetfulness' or 'jumbling things up' even though the victim's recollection is perfect.

3. **Diverting:** In this case, the gaslighter tries to divert the victim or make them question themselves by changing the topic of discussion. An example is "I'm sure your crazy sister told you to monitor my phone calls." Or "None of this is true, you're making them up to hurt me."

4. **Downplaying facts:** When the victim complains about an unsavory situation or expresses a fear, the gaslighter scoffs at the issue or downplays its seriousness, making the victim feel like a child with a tantrum. You hear phrases like "You're angry because of *that*?"

5. **Outright denial:** The gaslighter will deny promises that they made, outrightly telling the victim that they never said so and that the entire conversation happened in the victim's mind. For example, "I never told you to keep dinner waiting for me!"

6. **Pathologizing:** Especially cruel gaslighters may decide to play doctor with your mental health and 'diagnose' you of instability in a bid to cover up their own behavior. They can go on to make claims that you are 'unstable', 'not all there', 'spacey', or 'vengeful' in a bid to completely unhinge their victims. They may even advise you to book an appointment with a psychiatrist, all the while acting as if they are working for your best interest and thereby making

you believe that something is truly wrong with you.

7. **Discrediting:** A gaslighter will, under the guise of helping you, spread falsehoods and rumors about you to the people within your circle. They would pretend to be worried about you and use that opportunity to tell others that you are unstable or have been acting weird. They may also turn around to tell you that others think you are crazy as a way to drive a wedge between you and the people you would normally go to for help.

8. **Put blames on you:** A gaslighter will find a way to always blame you for whatever wrong they do. Make an attempt to have an important conversation about how they hurt you

and they will turn the discussion upside down that you will start believing that you are the reason for their bad behavior.

9. **Shaming:** Another tool the gaslighter uses in keeping the victim quiet is by subtly shaming them by making victims feel stupid about a fact that they have distorted. You will then apologize to them for speaking out about a bad behavior you called out when they have convinced you it's all in your head. A husband that has been cheating may turn the tables on you by saying: "I can't believe you would think that I would cheapen our relationship in that manner! If you believe I did this, it means *you* have been unfaithful to me," he might say.

10. **Use kind words to keep you off-guard:**
When you call out a gaslighter, they may surprise you by using kind words that may make you assume that maybe they are not so bad after all. But if they use kind words when confronted without changing their behavior or stopping the things that hurt you, they are only being manipulative because, after a while, you will start thinking that you are too emotional.

CHAPTER 2: Hidden Manipulations and How to Spot Them

The key to successfully gaslighting a person is to keep the victim off-balance, unsure, and without a sense of control. It is done so slowly, so subtly that the victim hardly realizes what is going on.

But it is possible to spot a pattern in the little ways a (potential) gaslighter tries to arrange situations in his favor. This is especially easy when you tune in to the way you feel when you are with someone. By paying attention and listening to yourself, you can easily know when someone is manipulating you with the intent to gaslight.

1) If you start doubting the way you feel or the things you see and keep trying to convince yourself that maybe you are just too sensitive, you may be a victim of gaslighting.

2) If you begin to doubt your judgment or ability to do something when you have always been capable in the past. You may even be afraid of saying what you feel or expressing yourself, especially if sharing your thoughts with that person in the past has eroded your confidence or led to confusion.

3) If you have feelings of vulnerability or insecurity that make you tiptoe around that person. You are afraid of 'rocking the boat' so you watch everything you say, do, and even your facial expressions. Realize that you are being gaslighted.

4) If you feel trapped or powerless and feel isolated from other people and the things going on around you. You may even believe that other people think that you are unstable or crazy just because a

particular person keeps telling you that you are.

5) If your friend/partner/relative's words make you feel like a stupid person that cannot do things right and you find that you are calling yourself by those abusive names.

6) If you are no longer happy with whom you are now compared to your past self. This is especially true if you realize that you are now afraid of the things that you used to be able to do in the past because you are no longer sure that you will succeed at it.

7) If your friend/partner/relative behaves inconsistently—the same thing they praised you for two days ago is what they are lashing out at you for now.

8) If your partner/friend/relative trivialize their hurtful actions or speech by making you feel like a child. For example: "Can't you take a joke? Geez, I was only kidding!"

9) If you experience feelings of impending doom or danger when you are with this person without any rational reason for feeling that way.

10) If you feel that you should apologize for every little thing especially about things related to who you are or your identity.

11) If you are no longer able to defend yourself or you are afraid of explaining your stand on issues.

12) If you feel that you are not as good as the other person and believe that anything they demand you do is a way of making you become better.

13) If you start doubting your memories and are no longer sure if you remember the past correctly—this may make you afraid to talk about the past because you fear that your memory is incorrect.

14) If you try your best to make the other person happy but feel that nothing you do will ever measure up to what they desire.

15) If you are unable to make decisions because you fear that you are not capable of seeing things clearly and would rather allow your friend/partner/relative decide for you.

16) If you are afraid that something is wrong with you even though there has been no evidence except the continued talks and berating of your friend/partner/relative.

CHAPTER 3: Why Does Gaslighting Work So Well?

You would think that with all the information available on gaslighting, it would be difficult to get caught in the web of this sort of abuse. But this is hardly the case as even educated and self-assured people have been victims of manipulators through gaslighting.

Here are some of the reasons why this abuse remains effective. Being aware of them can help you get out of it or prevent it from happening in the first place.

a) Gaslighting capitalizes on any little self-doubt a victim has about his/her abilities and then magnifies them. It also uses any trauma suffered in the past to make the victim feel unworthy and unsuitable to see things clearly.

b) It runs through the store of self-assurance a victim possesses such that they are no longer able to validate themselves but would rather give in to the gaslighter's supposed superior knowledge.

c) It erodes the victim's sense of worth and certainty about their values, beliefs, and worldview.

d) Gaslighting invents fears and insecurities that the victim does not possess and makes the victim concern about working on them instead of the gaslighter's behavior.

e) Gaslighting never allows the victim any leverage or a place to hide. A behavior that resulted in praises one day may bring about vituperation on another day.

CHAPTER 4: Dealing with Gaslighting

Gaslighting, like most forms of psychological abuses, is not easy to deal with. This is because it is very easy for the gaslighter to deny that the condition exists at all. If they keep making claims that 'it's all in your head', it becomes a sort of battle to even admit that the situation truly exists not to talk of working on it.

To effectively deal with gaslighting, you should understand where the gaslighter is coming from. Most gaslighters are hurting people—people that have been abused or deprived of attention while growing up. They need to be right always or else their low self-esteem issues come up.

Here are some ways by which you can address gaslighting.

i. **Recognize its pattern.**

Gaslighting is powerful because it is subtle. Much like an inexperienced diver that gets pulled in to see more and more exciting coral beds until they go in too deep, gaslighting pulls you in such that you may not quickly realize that it is happening. There is always an explanation on the gaslighter's part for the way you feel and if they are people you trust and respect, you may easily buy into their version of the truth. So, know the signs—the lying, the projecting, the use of kindness and flattery, turning people against you, etc. When you know the signs, you can quickly take steps to stop it once it starts.

ii. **Realize that it is not really about you.** Gaslighting seems like an attack on your person—your memories, feelings, emotions, and interests. This may make you automatically defensive but often, gaslighting has to do with an insecure person's need for control over another. A gaslighter never feels up-to-par unless they have the upper hand. There are a lot of inadequacies behind their persona of charisma and capability. Once you realize this, you may decide whether the relationship is worth maintaining (under a different set of rules, of course).

iii.   **Stop wishing things were different.**
When someone we know and trust
gaslights us, the instinctive reaction is
denial. ''No, he wouldn't hurt me this
way," "She would know this is not in my
best interest and stop," etc. It is easy to
keep hoping that logic will overrule their
behavior, that they will realize how they
are hurting you and change. This may
make you develop 'a tougher skin' and
continue to take the gaslighting. Throw
this wish into the trash, it may never
happen. Focus on your own emotional
health and getting better.

iv.   **Realize that they may never change.** Even in cases where the gaslighter was a victim of abuse or emotional deprivation in childhood, they may never become a better person. Appealing to their 'good nature' will hardly work but only draw you in deeper. Unless a gaslighter admits that something is wrong by themselves and decide to start therapy, they may never give up the behavior.

v.   **Choose defiance.**

Assertive people are more likely to survive gaslighting or come out quicker than unassertive people. When you refuse to bend over to the gaslighter's will, it becomes easier to trust in your own reality. Children with parents that were gaslighters were able to survive because they chose defiance and what they knew to be true rather than assuming that 'Mother/Father knows best.'

vi. **Keep records:**

A gaslighter will make you a promise, renege on it, then turn around to blame you for getting it wrong. Let's say you are working on a particularly big project at work and your gaslighting boss has promised you an incentive if you attain a certain benchmark at a particular time. You hit the target within the specified time frame only for your boss to not to say anything about the promised incentive. You approached him only for him to insist that the conversation never took place. This is where keeping record will help. If you get the incentive promise in writing or insisted on an email to that effect, it will serve as a backup for you.

vii.   **Get a life:**

Gaslighters love being the most important people in a room. They will make everything about you inconsequential and make theirs of importance. Do not allow them to dismiss anything that concerns you. Your job (be it a mail clerk or a surgeon) matters, your hobby is important and anything you do for self-care is not frivolous. So go out and do the things that you love no matter what the gaslighter thinks. If they belittle it, do not try to justify it but just continue. As you take a stand by fighting for the things that matter to you, the gaslighter may realize that your needs are as valid as theirs.

viii. **Consider cutting off the gaslighter.**

Because gaslighting is usually perpetrated by someone close to us, you may find yourself looking for a way to keep hold of the relationship while trying to escape the gaslighting. But this is not always possible; some gaslighters will only get worse and worse and the only way to maintain/regain your sanity is to have them completely out of your life. Find another job if your boss or line manager is gaslighting you, change your denomination if it's coming from a religious leader, end a relationship if the culprit is a boyfriend/girlfriend. Choose yourself first, always.

ix.   **Never second-guess yourself.**

You have trusted your instinct all your life, why should you now believe someone else over what your instinct tells you? So if you begin to doubt your instincts, ask yourself what your heart tells you is going on. Try to keep notes of things that happen so that you can have a solid proof of facts to back up your feelings. And as long as you have not allowed yourself to be isolated, it is always a good idea to ask other people outside of your relationship with the gaslighter, their opinion on issues that bother you.

x.   **Have a solid support system:**

We all need people for emotional support from time to time but a victim of gaslighting needs this much more than others. When the gaslighter continually tries to skew your perspective and make you question what you see, you need some people to help you confirm your reality and assure you that you are okay. Do not believe any false claim that the gaslighter is the only person that cares about you, that others cannot be bothered. Keep up with all your other relationships and tell them what is going on.

xi. **Build up your self-worth.**

Words are powerful and it is possible to start believing all the lies of the gaslighter—that you are not capable of doing great things, that you are pathetic, a slob, not good at managing money, etc. So, help yourself by remembering the times in the past when you were grounded and capable and positive. Remind yourself that you are a wonderful person that deserves to be loved.

xii. **Never get defensive with a gaslighter.**

It is quite difficult to keep your cool when you are faced with a lair but that is what you should do with a gaslighter. When you start arguing with them, they will turn the tables on you and call you 'crazy', 'hysterical', or 'emotional'. And the more agitated you get, the more it seems that the gaslighter is telling the truth.

xiii.   **Get professional help:**

Once you no longer have confidence in
your thoughts or feelings, you need to
seek out a therapist for help. You should
be able to trust your own judgment
about situations concerning you or
around you but the moment you start
second-guessing that as a result of
someone always telling you that you:
overreact, are emotional, 'get it wrong',
etc., you are already in more trouble than
you thought.

You may ask the gaslighter to get
help too, especially if they are
someone that you are in a romantic
relationship with or whom you are
not ready to cut out of your life yet.
Through therapy, you will be able to

shore up your self-esteem that has been eroded by criticisms and poisonous talks.

xiv. **Walk away.**

One thing that every victim of gaslighting needs to understand is that this is one time that it is absolutely okay to be selfish. You have the right to prioritize your mental health over everything else and you should, too. If you try to make a gaslighter see the damage that they are doing but they refuse to change, you should cut them out of your life. It does not matter if they are your parents, spouse, friends, boss or mentor. Severe the relationship and do not look back.

You do not even need to explain to them why you are walking away (they will find a way to make it your fault), you just do. Let them know that the relationship is no longer serving you and walk away. Block them on social media, block their calls from coming into your phone, ignore emails and do not pick calls coming from unknown numbers.

CHAPTER 5: Mindfulness: A tool for dealing with gaslighting

Mindfulness is your ability to be fully present and aware of where you are and what you are doing. It involves being in tune with all your senses (sight, hearing, taste, smell, touch) per time. When you are fully grounded by being aware through the use of your senses, it acts as a countering effect to gaslighting which seeks to distort your reality. By being present, a gaslighter will find it difficult to convince you of a fabricated wrongdoing, make you accept a distorted truth, or trivialize their bad behavior.

Here are ways through which you can become more mindful and quickly recognize gaslighting for what it is.

a) **Boost your instinct.** The intuition or instinct is a primal feeling of rightness or wrongness about something without the use of proof, evidence, knowledge, or reasoning. It gives you important information about situations and people. So learn to listen to your gut, the more you listen to it, the more efficient it becomes. It can tell you whom to trust without, warn you of dangerous situations, advise on a business decision, or prevent you from making mistakes. Because one of the easiest ways to gaslight is by making a victim doubt himself (and his feelings), being in tune with your gut will cue you in to when you are being served a load of bull.

b) **Journaling.** This is an effective way of keeping track of conversations, promises made, and occurrences. By having a record of the things that go on in your life, you can tune in quickly when something is 'off.' And when you write down the conversations you had with a gaslighter, you will be able to preserve your sanity when they turn around and deny what they said.

c) **Meditate.** When you meditate, you learn to observe your thoughts and feelings, to see the little things that shape your decisions and acknowledge them. During a meditation session, all your focus is on your body: your body scan, breathing, emotions, etc. and this helps you to develop your attention muscle so that you become quickly attuned to a gaslighter's distracting techniques and can quickly call it out.

d) **Engage in Mind-Body Practices.** Any activity that brings your mind and body in sync is an antidote to gaslighting.

Yoga, meditation, Tai Chi all link your mind with your body and prevent you from the disconnection that comes with being gaslighted. They also protect you from stress and PTSD that may come with gaslighting.

CHAPTER 6: How to Recover from Gaslighting

Gaslighting is capable of leaving emotional scars on its victims. Its effects do not just go away with an end to the gaslighting. So, learn how you can recover from it and go ahead to live your best life.

a) **Go out with friends.** If the gaslighter tried to turn your friends against you, now is the time to renew those friendships. So turn to the people who love you and believe in you as a person. Go out and enjoy their company, laugh and be happy. Get in touch with what it means to be a complete individual.

b) **Do something useful.** One of the effects of gaslighting is the powerlessness that comes with it. Someone who cannot trust their own instincts will naturally shy away from anything that gives them a measure of control over anybody. So go out and do something: take a road trip, travel abroad, teach little kids a skill, start a DIY. The sense of accomplishment you will get from successfully completing a project will wipe away the insecurities caused by the gaslighting.

c) **Address any depression.** It is possible to fall into depression after being gaslighted for a long time. You, therefore, need to address any of the effects that you may be experiencing. Seek professional help if you have difficulty concentrating, have lost appetite, find it difficult to sleep, or are unable to complete tasks. Do not turn to alcohol or drugs to numb the effects of depression.

d) **Safety first.** In a situation where you decided to cut off all ties with a gaslighter and they are not ready for the relationship to end, you need to take steps to ensure your physical safety. Move away from where they are especially if you are afraid they may get violent—and get a restraining order if you have to. Change your phone lines and install caller ID to be able to recognize if they try to call. If you post on social media, desist from tagging your location or mentioning where you are.

CHAPTER 7: Self-care Strategies for Combating Gaslighting

The secret to preventing or recovering from being gaslighted is to have a very strong sense of self. This can be built by taking time out to do the things that make you healthy physically, mentally, and emotionally. Here are activities to incorporate into your life in fighting gaslighting:

1. **Become attuned to what your body is telling you.** The fast pace and pressures of the world we live in means that most of the time, we do not take time to listen to ourselves. So start listening to whatever your body tells you. Begin with listening and taking appropriate actions when you are hungry, fatigued, or thirsty. As you take the right action to the right feeling, you will gradually realize that your instincts are valid; you can trust

them. Believe that as your judgment about when to eat is valid, so also is your judgment about weightier things that you may need to decide on.

2. **Verify what you see.** After a season of doubting the things that your eyes tell you, it may be difficult to believe them a hundred percent. Use the people you trust to confirm what you see or are told. The people that have always had your back can help you with confirming the things you know or what someone else (that you are not sure of) told you.

3. **Start positive self-affirmations:** New Age gurus are so much into self-affirmations for one simple reason—they work so well. To recover your sense of self-worth, write a list of all the great qualities you possess, all the people that

love you, and all the projects you have worked on and use it to affirm why you are strong, beautiful, valuable, capable, etc. Repeat this time and time again as your feelings of worthlessness try to creep in.

4. **Renew interest in a hobby.** Being a victim of gaslighting has probably disengaged you from the things that bring joy to your life. Now is the time to go back to them. Your gaslighter might have derided your interest in painting, telling you that you are not good enough and will never amount to anything. Now is the time to pick it up again and do it for the joy it gives you. Allot a portion of time each day to the thing(s) that make you happy and do them. Do not mind

how frivolous or childish your interest might seem, just do it.

5. **Eat right.** One of the emotional responses to gaslighting could be overeating or under eating. Whatever side you were on, now is the time to take care of what you eat. Cut out all junk foods and go for healthy, whole foods like fruits, vegetables, whole grains, poultry, and healthy fats. Address all issues of emotional eating or numbing with alcohol. As you eat the right foods, your mood will naturally improve and your sense of self with increase.

6. **Work out.** Start going to the gym or take up running. Register for a yoga class, Tai Chi, or Zumba. You might have neglected your physical health because the gaslighter deemed it unimportant

but you should now make it a priority. By working out, you gain energy and sharpen your focus. The fitter you get, the more difficult it is for you to fall into the role of a victim.

7. **Build your tribe.** Your tribe is those people that will be there for you no matter what, that will always trust your judgment and want the best for you. So rebuild your relationship with family and friends especially if the gaslighter has alienated them from you. Spend time one-on-one with family and friends, let them get to know you again. Honor invitations to parties, weekends away, and road trips. As you surround yourself with the people that love you, you gain strength in yourself and your abilities anew.

8. **Get professional help.** A trained therapist will be able to listen to you without judgment and help you heal faster. They will also be able to address any anxiety or depression you might be feeling by offering you treatment options to regain your emotional and psychological health. Do not feel any shame in having being gaslighted; share with them openly to enable them to aid you in dealing with the effects of the gaslighting.

Important Note

No matter how long you have been gaslighted, it is possible to come out of it and regain your sense of self. The first thing to do is to identify the gaslighting and realize that you are not to blame. Decide to stop being a victim and work on increasing your emotional awareness. But practicing mindfulness, you can become more attuned to how you feel and learn to trust your reality against what a gaslighter may tell you. Get the help of a certified psychologist, turn to family and friends, and engage in activities that bring you joy. If a complete break from the gaslighter will ensure your healing, do not be afraid to walk away, close that door and throw away the key.

Other Books by The Same Author

Change Your Life: How to Overcome Anxiety, Depression and Negative Thinking

Anxiety and Phobia Workbook: How to Overcome Anxiety and Panic Attacks

How to Deal with Difficult People: Control the Situation! Overcome Your Annoying and Frustrating Coworkers, Friends, Parents, or Classmates

How to Overcome Shyness and Social Anxiety: Deal with Stage Fright, Fear of Public Speaking, Social Phobia, And Ultimately Gain New Confidence

How to Deal with Rejection: Powerful Ways to Restore Social Confidence, Attract Better Opportunities, And Take Charge of Your Environment

How to Deal with A Narcissist: Best Ways to Respond to A Narcissist,

Confront Self-Important People, And
Thrive Efficiently

Anger Management Techniques: How to
Control Outbursts, Frustration, &
Depression Using Emotional Intelligence

Printed in Great
Britain
by Amazon